# WHISPERS IN THE SHADOWS

# THE ART OF CHIAROSCURO

## Nicole Maharaj

BookLeaf
Publishing

India | USA | UK

Whispers In The Shadows © 2021 Nicole Maharaj

All rights reserved.

No part of this publication may be reproduced, stored in a retrieval system, or transmitted, in any form or by any means, electronic, mechanical, photocopying, recording or otherwise, without the prior written permission of the presenters.

Nicole Maharaj asserts the moral right to be identified as author of this work.

Presentation by *BookLeaf* Publishing

Web: www.bookleafpub.com

E-mail: info@bookleafpub.com

ISBN: 9789358361940

First edition 2021

# DEDICATED TO

the shadows of my memories that are never far behind me

# ACKNOWLEDGEMENT

"These poems at heart have been inspired by many failed crushes on people I have never had the courage to face. For all those, it may include I am thankful to all of you because you have shaped the person that I am today. I am also grateful for my friends and family who have always pushed me to never stop writing or give up on my passion."

# PREFACE

"In the world we live in today, we often embark on challenges to make the everyday different. I have always written and since November 2020 I have been inspired to write articles or fiction everyday. I embarked on the journey to write a poem a day to see if I could do it, and I did, and relearned my love for verse all at the same time. I chose to theme my poetry in the art of Chiaroscuro, the effect of using light and shadow in art. Light and the dark are with us everyday, you can't have one without the other just like you can't have a poison without an antidote. We have all lived separate from each other, the pandemic a poison to the very lives of us all. There has to be an antidote to this poison, I've found peace with these poems in a dark time of the world, hopefully other people will too."

# 1. THE PATH

"They walked down the path,

hand in hand,

secrets hidden

in their eyes,


The world at their feet,

They did not fear

the future,


Or the past

that still seemed to

cling to them

with grasping hands,

that turned to

an all-consuming darkness

Life had not been

kind to them


So they weren't kind to it

They cared not for the people

or the children of the world.

For when had they ever cared for them?


Until the day

that their hands separated,

one path turned to two.

Their hands changed.

Their minds with it,

gone was the

scared boy clinging

to his mother.


The man was cold,

and tired of the World's atrocities,

He paved a world for himself,

devoid of splendor,

or beauty.


Just the all-consuming darkness,

and the monsters that had long plagued

him.


A world that belonged to him alone.

For the path

He walked was one of darkness.

devoid of light.


His loved ones gone,

and yet he still walked,

the endless

Path "

## 2. A CURIOUS PEOPLE

"In a town,

deep in a shadowy

Vale,

There lived a great many people,

These people

did not bother

with much,

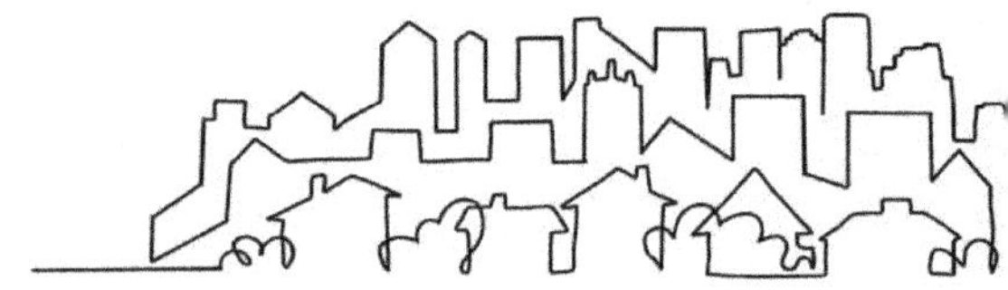

so there was

much that did

not bother

them,

This Town was a curious thing,

full of curious

people,

I had happened

upon them

quite by

accident.

But that is how

an Unexpected

Journey

Truly begins

When you aren't

looking for

Trouble

Content with

where life has taken

you,

It was at one of

those moments where

I came to be

in a sort of trouble

the one that can become

all-consuming,


should you let it?

So I ran.

And ran.


Ending up in a shadowy

vale

surrounded by a,

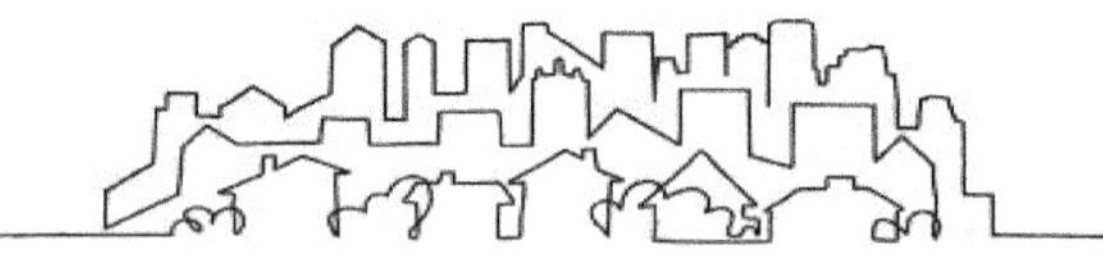

Curious people

who was led by

a

serious man.

Just as curious

as the people he

led. "

# 3. ONE DAY

"Perhaps one day,

I will forget what you look like.

How it felt when you

held me.


When I once

belonged to you

Now I belong to

no one.


Perhaps I never will.


Maybe one day

someone else's

kiss

will erase the memory of

yours.

Maybe one day someone

will look at me

the way you

once did.

Maybe one day

I won't be lost in

the moment

that moment

I'll have other

stolen

Midnight moments

Perhaps one day

I will know true love.

Not this

one sided love

that lasted

for but a moment

for you.

Leaving me with memories,

wishes,

hopes,

and wants.


Always the wanting.

Of things that will

never be.


For you belong to

someone else,

and

I belong to

no one. "

# 4. TWIN SUNS

"Twin suns followed,

me through the

darkness

Shadows receding,

from where they had

lain dormant in

my heart



It takes but a single moment

a single sun

to bring light

to where there was only

darkness



Such a deep darkness

that seemed to swallow me

whole



I had loved once

but even that had been

a sham

so I went back into

the dark



The ever lonely

darkness

until the two suns

came

they came with

bravery

and love

To show me all the ways
to banish the darkness

and step into the

light


I was happy for once

hopeful for once

in the bask

of the twin suns,

those suns,

Born out of a

never-ending darkness

that was

mine."

# 5. INTO THE DARK

"Dark in the deep

where no one

dares to enter,

there is a man

who has hidden

from the world,

from the treacheries

of man,

from the coldness

of women,

from the weakness of children.


He chose to stay away

for safety

for peace

from never-ending

pressures of a world

with no peace,

A world always on the

brink of war,


He had never expected

anyone to find

him

there

deep in the dark


Hidden from the world

or so he thought


They came with

anger,

and with so much sorrow

they talked of the end of the

world

but the man had lived long

and knew that the world

would endure

no matter what end it faced

but now they wanted him

to rejoin the world

to fight

and regain the earth

from the people

who would see it go

to nothing.

There was no choice

but to live or to die

he wanted to say no

but he couldn't

not when faced with

her,


and the eyes

that reminded him

of someone lost long ago,

so now he was lost

doomed to go up to the sky

and save the world

once again. "

# 6. THE LIGHT

"There was a light

that shone through

the darkness,

it banished it

through the trees

things that had

been scary

once


Were lit up in the light

that seemed to come

from nowhere

and everywhere,

 all

at once

That's how she was found.


The lost princess,

now found.


The light had

searched through

the darkness to find her

before it would be

too late


and there she was

on the ground

like the princess she had always been

Away from the prying eyes

of the royals

who would subjugate her

and the forest friends

that had tried to keep

her with them
20


The light now took her

for itself

out of the darkness

out of the forest

into the light,

of a never ending,

Dawn "

# 7. TIME PASSES

"Time passes

as it does

everything

Through the clouds,

The sun,

the wind

the sky.

The girl with

sunrises in her eyes

and constellations in her hair

drank in the air

the wind,

the sky,

as she pondered the intricacies of

life

of time passing

and wondered

if today was the day,

 she had waited

for

or if today would

be another day of

waiting


Always waiting

for a day that

will never

come

a moment

away

from the terribleness of

a world on the

brink "

# 8. FOOTSTEPS

23

"Footsteps

Made a path

Through the

Forest

Around the lake

Into the gale,

The night before,

We met

They seemed to

Tell our story

Of whispered moments,

In love filled

Mornings

The hushed

Kisses of the dark

The whispers of

Lovers in the morning

I have waited for

You

The way you

Have waited for

Me.

Yearning for

One last touch

One last kiss,

One last moment,

In a lover's embrace

But like the night,

Before we met,

Those footsteps

Came

And took me away

From love,

From joy

From hope

To a never ending

Despair

Away from

Every lovers

Touch

Ever happy lover's

Moment.


The Dawn

Fading into

An even

Deeper

Darkness

Of no

Return"

# 9. THE VOW



"I had once met

a man

who was on the

run,

He had done

something

once

a

long

time ago,

When he was a

different man,

but a man

just the same

he had made my heart

beat

outside my

chest

The first

stirrings of love,

until he disappeared

never to be seen


Until one day circumstances

brought us together

to journey

a Quest

a failure of

escape


He had vowed

sometime on this

journey

that he would always

keep me safe

and warm


I should've known

that vow

would mean his death

and so I watched him

fall to his doom

helpless to help

this lone man of

mine.

As he fell

I returned back to

the woman I had

once been

A woman safe

a  woman like no other

a woman who had once loved

a man

on the

run. "

# 10. HOPE

"In the absence of

hope,

there is a void

darker

than the

deepest

dark


Where roam the

broken hearted

the bereft

the ones that have


no hope

no faith

no perseverance

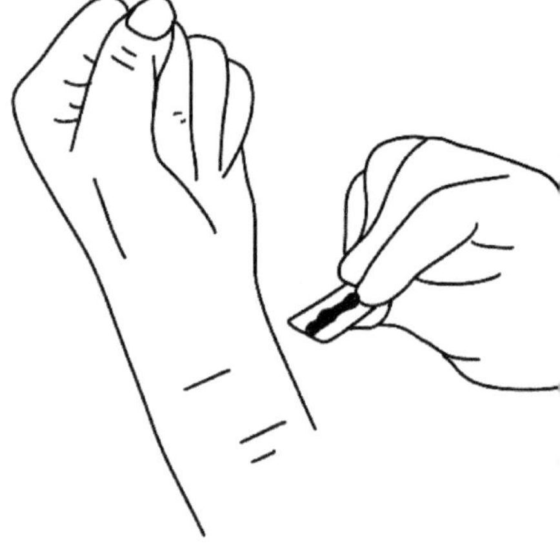

that anything will

be the same again



Without hope

there is despair

there is loss

so profound

it eats you

up



swallows you whole

Makes everything

seem like the

hardest thing

you would

ever do.



This is where the

princess of time

lived

not because she wanted

but because she had to


Time was a cancer

the bitterest moments

must hold

a fascination

for those who

did not feel


So as the Princess

of time she

guarded those

bitter moments

those hopeless dreams

in the shadow

of the realm of Hades



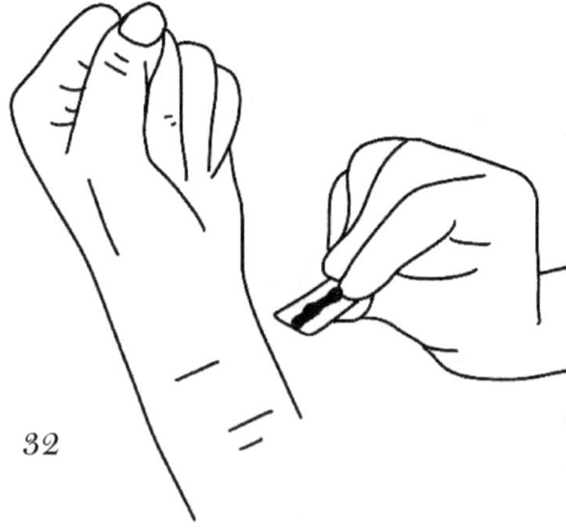

forever waiting

for a single moment

to be released from her

duty



to see the wonder

and happiness of the

world,



if there was such a thing

beyond the void

of never-ending

circumstance

Of a life filled

without hope. "

# 11. ONE DANCE

"Like the start

of a slow song

It started with

the beat of the

drums

The slide of fabric

rustling,

Hands touching

Fingers locking

A dip

Long curls

cascading

down her

back

A thousand memories

sparked by a single

moment


A thousand lifetimes

in a single look

A moment in time

that would last

forever


Holding close

what would

forever slip

out of his

grasp


She didn't belong to him

She wasn't his

Like he wasn't

hers

They only had this

moment


This dance

before their last

goodbye

as sorrowful

as their

first hello


Always destined to

part

Never to be

one

Not this lifetime

or the next

Just one more

Moment

One more

dance


Until they part

Once again "

# 12. YOUNG LOVE

"It started from

the first look

the first touch

the first shy utterance


Their eyes met across

the path

across the schoolroom,

across the dark theater

A single glance

that seemed to show

a thousand lifetimes,


Lifetimes that will never be

for people too shy

to look at each other

too shy to speak to

each other

will never be


But that's what happens

with young love,

a brief moment

that never lasts

a brief touch that

seems to make

everything worthwhile


Until it vanishes in the

next moment,

to another love,

a deeper love


Young love never lasts

it always changes

until the first heartbreak

that grows you into a more

adult love


A lasting love,

till the end of time."

# 13. WORDS I'LL NEVER BE ABLE TO SAY

"The first time I saw you

I was intimidated

but I forced

myself to say Hi,


and that first time you spoke to me,

I knew you would never hurt me,

Since then,

I have learned that you are,

Unbearably kind and sweet.


That you were kind of person

I would never want to stop

talking to.

Your laugh makes me blush.

Your smile makes me laugh.

You are savage and sarcastic

and have so many unique views

of the world.


When you 're near

I'm never bored,

When you're not,

 I can't stop

thinking and talking about you


My day is not complete unless

I've spoken to you at least once


But I will never know if I'll be able to tell you how I feel.

Because I'd rather have you in my

life as a friend,

Then say goodbye forever. "

# 14. THE LONELY HEARTS CLUB

"A broken heart

is something

easily shared

each heart in

love with another

most seducing

love.

Two hearts

don't always

become one

some loves too toxic too

last.

Love and Lust

being confused

for the other

misunderstandings

abound in the

world.


People change

just as circumstances

does


Once in love,

turns to hate

or friendship.


Love and friendship

can be confused for

the other.


A thousand lifetimes,
in a single

glance.

A thousand

heartbreaks in a

single sentence.


To love

and be loved

is a curse

all in itself.

Embraces

are from the heart,

Friendships can turn

love into hate

and back against.


Nothing ever stays

the same

in this world,

full of maybes

and No's


People of all,

colors and types

can make everyone be

confused

make everyone's

heartbreak

and join

The

Lonely Hearts Club. "

## 15. FOR YOUR LOVE

"Trying to gain your

attention

is like trying to

grasp water

both things

it seems

nearly impossible

in front of

the other


You look at me

and my heart

stutters in my

chest

Words come out

all wrong

and all I can

seem to do

is the

exact wrong thing


Gaining your love

is the most impossible

thing


The only thing

being possible

is watching you

love someone else

fall in love

with everyone

but me


Loving someone is easy

but gaining that love

almost impossible. "

# 16. TWO BROKEN HEARTS

50

"There were once

two travelers

on the road less

traveled

they both had

journeyed there

out of nowhere

all hope gone

all love in their

heart shattered

beyond belief.

They had been

friends once

a long time

ago

Before autumn

winds swept

their hopes

and dreams upon

another

before the winter winds

spread their  wings


At last they looked

up and saw each other

in the midst of a summer

dream


Looking like their old friend

of fate


Their destiny to be the last in the shadows

As they traveled

the road less traveled

with sore hearts

and heads full of

sorrow

.

Two hearts broken

in the worlds

darkest

vale."

# 17. FOLLOWING THE FOOTSTEPS

"In the steps of someone

I had known a lifetime before

I've seen her

in times of sadness

in happier times

when there seems

to be a little more hope

in the world

She had always been my

mirror,

the way I wanted to

represent myself

in the world.

My shadow self

the better half

of my soul

that appeared

every so often

in the barest glimmer

of my more braver

moments.


Was she a real person

or just someone

that I followed

or just shadows

of all the people

I've loved the best


People in our lives

come and go

they leave imprints on you,

footsteps that you

can follow

traits that you

can aspire to

have


Dreams to follow

steps to walk in

Love that you can always

share

Memories that fade in time

but will never be truly forgotten

no matter how

embarrassing

sad,

or crazy

it will always be remembered

with love,

Following the Footsteps

in memory. "

# 18. BROKEN DREAMS

"Broken dreams and Shattered Hearts,

Fill the hallowed Vale,

We had once happened upon here

When we were young and

Filled with hope

And restless dreams,

Havoc is all that life is,

Havoc and sorrow that fills this

Vale

With broken dreams and shattered hearts

All scattered in the vale

We have waked here once before

In a nightmare or two

The bogeyman always appears

And tries to entice us to stay

But we learned long ago never

To follow a man of darkness such as

He,

We knew once of the Shadow man in the

Darkness of the vale

Now we stare into the sun to rid ourselves

Of the stark loneliness

Of the vale full of

Shattered hearts

And

Broken Dreams "

# 19. THERE WAS A KNOCK ON THE DOOR

"It was about midday

When there was a knock on the

Door,

In the house with the green door

And the childlike man

Ran to the fan,

That stood by the door,

Around the moor,

He was dismayed to find

Guests

At his door,

For it was his fate

To guard the gate,

That led to a grate

Oh what a fate,

To guard the grate,

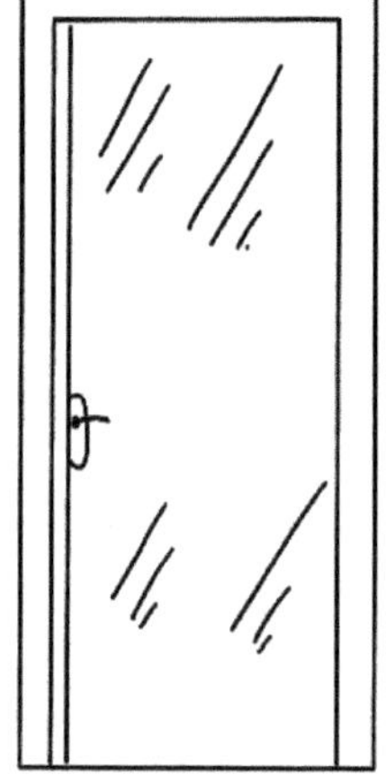

To the door

By the moor,

Where another man stood

Guarding the gate. "

# 20. THE WAVES

"The waves crash against the shore,

The foam gathering in thick bubbles

On the floor,

Covering the toes of giggling children

Playing on the shore,

Laughing parents watch over

 their children as they lay

in the shade.


Far off in the deep water,

Mermaids swim along the fishes,

Enjoying the treasures that lay on

The floor of the ocean,

From long ago sea voyages,

From Britain to Spain,

The sea is a main source of

Pain,

As the waves crash on the floor,

On the edge of the cave."

"Thunder shook the ground,

As the King knelt on the mound,

His knights surrounded him,

As they stood vigil,

Against the rising moon.


The Queen to approach on the coming,

Rise of the tide,

Light suffused the Sky,

In violet and Blue,

An unholy magic

For an unholy woman.


The Queen and Sorceress

One in the same. "

www.ingramcontent.com/pod-product-compliance
Lightning Source LLC
LaVergne TN
LVHW050930200726
843508LV00011B/2303